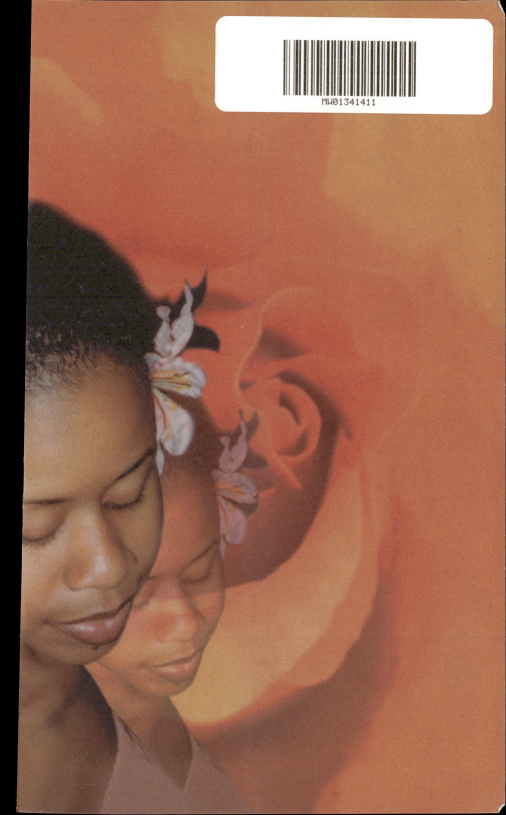

Heart Love Messages of the Soul

by
Sherehe
Yamaisha
Rozé

Heart Love Messages of the Soul, Second Edition

Copyright © 2002, 2010 by Sherehe Yamaisha Rozé Hollins

Written and illustrated by Sherehe Yamaisha Rozé Hollins

Cover art by Khaleedah Ishé Hollins, Reginald Hailey and Steve Manczuk

Book design by Jan Carpenter Tucker, J.L. Carpenter Design

All rights reserved. No part of this book may be reproduced by any mechanical, photographic, or electronic process, or in the form of a phonographic recording; nor may it be stored in a retrieval system, transmitted, or otherwise be copied for public or private use—other than for "fair use" as brief quotations embodied in articles and reviews—without prior written permission of the publisher.

Published by Heart Love Publications, San Diego, California

ISBN 978-0-9822432-1-3

Printed in the United States of America

Heart Love Messages of the Soul

Second Edition

by
Sherehe Yamaisha Rozé

Heart Love Publications

*This book is dedicated to
My Family,
whose love and inspiration
continue to guide my creativity.
~ Love everlasting*

Rose Carolyn England Lewis
December, 1931 - June, 1988
Grandma Rosie

Immortal Magnificence

A budding beauty smiles softly
With delicate petals as tender as silk.
And embraced by the heavens gently
Lies liberated in nature's quilt
With words of wisdom
To cure a heart that's wilt.
A beloved blossom beaming brightly.
My guardian until ages old,
As an angel's soft sweet soul.

Possessing stunning beauty
Adored by all whose eyes it met.
And for it the sun glistens
And at night the stars appear.
Wish all could last forever
But for night the day must set.
With petals bowed to kiss the earth
In gratitude sincere.
Dew posed upon the petal
Like a gently falling tear.

Soul ascends to heaven
Spirit's presence will protect.
Although gone, but not deceased
My sweet Rose
Rest in peace.

Contents

My Family	3
Mi Familia	6
She	9
Pink Tights for Cocoa Caramel Chocolate Colored Skin	12
Me 'n Poetry	14
Loving Me	15
Mama's Like	18
I Cry	22
Call to the Brothas	26
400 Years of Lynching and Counting	29
Question	32
Black on Black Love	35
Only When It's Dark Enough Can You See the Stars	38
I Am	41
Somos Una Gente	46
About the Author	50

First there was the nommo, or the word, and a thought became a thing.

~ *African Proverb*

Great Aunt Kate, who was born on a plantation in Missouri in 1880. She lived to be 100 and died four days before I was born, on my mother's birthday. She is the reason my mother teaches.

My Family

My Family,
sweet blessed.
You are the ones that give me strength
and make each day worth living.
Your precious gifts and generous hearts
illustrate love's true definition.
Your funny ways and laughter are why I smile.
Your pain is mine and so I cry.
Your ceaseless strength has built my path for success.
Because of you I know the value and importance of life.

This is My Family

Beautiful faces illuminating radiance,
invite the sun on my coldest day,
then hold out their hands and point the way.
At times distant like the branch and the root,
yet they depend upon each other and so birth the fruit.
Through clouds, rain, and thunder,
still there's us who can't be torn asunder.
Your bravery, your brilliance have helped me shine
and words of wisdom bring me peace of mind.

This is My Family

As delicate and lovely as my Rose,
I love you, I thank you for helping me grow.
You are the greatest gift I'll ever need.
You've laid the foundation
now I'll set myself free.
Soaring on to endless heights,
for what you've done
one can pay no price.
You've given me love.
You've blessed me with life.
MY FAMILY.

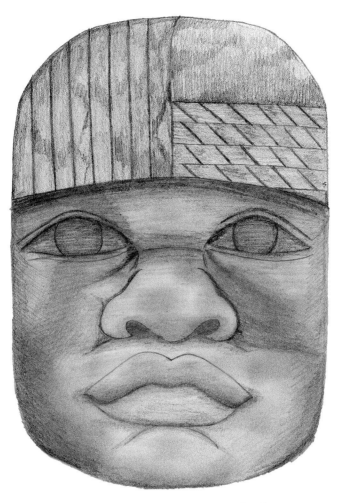

Olmec heads of Southern Mexico and Central America are a reminder of Africa's ancient presence in the Americas.

Mi Familia

Mí Familia,
dulce bendición.
Ustedes son los que me dan fuerza
y hacen que cada día valga la pena vivir.
Sus regalos preciosos y corazones generosos
ilustran la verdadera definición del amor.
Sus formas graciosas y risa es la razon por la que sonrío.
Su dolor es mi dolor y lloro.
Su inumerable fuerza ha construido mi camino,
hacía el suceso.
Por ustedes yo se el valor y la importancia de la vida.

Esta es Mí Familia

Rostros hermosos iluminados y radiantes,
invitan al sol en mis días mas frios,
y con sus manos muestran el camino.
A veces distanciados como la rama y la raíz,
pero aun asi dependen el uno del otro.
Entre nubes, lluvia, y truenos,
todavia estamos nosotros,
que no podemos ser separados.
Su valentía, su inteligencia,
me han ayudado a brillar.
Y palabras de sabiduría me
traen paz de mente.

Esta es Mí Familia

Los ámo y les agradezco
por ayudarme a crecer.
Ustedes son el regalo más grande
que necesitaré.
Ustedes han puesto la base
y ahora me liberare,
volando a grandes alturas.
Por lo que han hecho
no se quede pagar un precio.
Me han dado amor.
Me han bendecido con vida.
MÍ FAMILIA.

She

She's
reeeeeeeal
hot.
She ignites rhythms
that melt like butter
between saucy beats.
Soulful harmonies
melt like honey
between her lips.
Each drip
slowly slips
down your throat
into sweet bliss.
This Black Magic Woman
whispers words in the wind
that make autumn tree leaves dance.
With each breath she takes flight
like fire flies twinkling
against a summer's midnight.
She was born a Superstar.
Creator made her,
Great mother
molded
of red tierra clay,
Painted by golden dust
of Saharan sands and African sunlit skies.

She, Ancient Original, nestles the stars
within her breasts, carries the sun within
her womb, cultivates seeds of wisdom and truth
in her mind. Then births them into song, poetic
liberation psalms. *She*, Warrior Princess,
walks as liberated woman, with power
fierce yet graceful. *She* be victorious,
poised a regal lioness. Wearing
beauty at her waist side,
with head held high.
She be victoriously
transcending space
and time. To rise a
delicate lotus,
petals
soft, pure and perfect.
She, who naturally be so fine,
Is blessed in each breath
with Creator's nectar wine.
The fruit she bears
through voice
fulfills her purpose
One Most High.
She no one can define,
yet she calls
herself,
Divine.

*For
Arthur Mitchell,
creator of
Dance Theatre
of Harlem.*

Pink Tights for Cocoa Caramel Chocolate Colored Skin

He say pink tights
Don't go wit no cocoa caramel chocolate
colored skin
So he reach within his Black magic mind
Paints them brown
And revolutionizes rhythm
Spinning pirouettes to James Brown's
"Say it loud, I'M BLACK AND I'M PROUD."

Africa's hips sway to create a soul jazz ballet.
Graceful pliés accented by the snap of a hip
Grip the floor, moving feet to the beat of blues.
Arms spread like eagles' wings
Travel through space
To remember a time when Black
meant bad skin
And big behinds were not fit
For a ballerina's tutu and pink tights.

But dance is back in Black on Black bodies
Putting the soul back in rhythm
Liberating Black legs to rise
From every ghetto like butterflies
In celebration of *the dance*
Created by cocoa caramel chocolate colored people.

Me 'n Poetry

I create lyrical melodies
That hum bass drums
Sing harp strums
Tongue talk so fast
I scat rhymes
like Dinah Washington
Tones be trumpet horns
for Miles Davis
Lyrics spin Love Supremes
for John Coltrane
Rhymes come blessed en inglés
Y español
Y echo timbales
Por Tito Puente y su son
My pen salsas across the page
Like Congolese hips sway
'Cause music be me in poetry!

Loving Me

As a child,
I was taught
to stuff my breasts
inside tiny wire coated cups
so they would not draw too much attention.

There

hidden
behind cotton lining
constricted by elastic straps
I forgot about my sacred brown breasts

that dress my chest
like heavenly mountains,
that some days bow graciously to kiss the earth.

There

tucked inside tiny cups.
I forgot how they are soft like satin to touch.
How they joyfully bounce to the rhythm of their own beat
as I walk down the street.

There

shoved between
two pieces of wire and a bow
I forgot through my breasts flows nature's sweetness.

Along came adolescence.
My young mind trapped inside
man's perception of excellence.

Made me enhance my bust
with push up cups, which took me from A to B,
sometimes C, skipping sizes in between.

I just wanted to be perky
Even though it defeated the law of gravity,
'Cause God created me to hang low naturally.

So now that I'm grown
I know I must embrace me,

Rejoice in the sacredness
of my authenticity.

Regardless of whether my breasts
be big or small

I give thanks and praise and
accept it all!

*Mama Starla
at four years old.*

Mama's Like

Mama's like
A soulful church hymn singing
This Little Light of Mine.

Mama's like
her three sunkisses
shining sweetness
through rhythm and rhyme.

Mama's like
love on a sunny day
illuminating me with her smile.

Mama's like
a freedom song dancin' in the rain.

Mama's like
a spiritual guardian
guiding my ascendance.

Mama's like
a silent thunderstorm,
and Mama's my awakening,
'cause

Mama's like
tired of beatin' hands on dirty dishes
after a looong day's work.

Mama's like
    beans and corn bread with extra sop up.

Mama's like
    enchiladas, burritos, tacos
        con extra guacamole and a special touch
        of Africa.

Mama's like
    chili on a rainy day,
        and when the sun comes out to play,

Mama's like
    Rainbows.

Mama's like
    my *Ribbon in the Sky*
        and I am her *Cherie Amour*, as she
        softly sings me into sweet dreams.

Mama's like
    Patty Cake, Pee Pie, Little Sally Walker
    and *Jump Back Baby Jump Back.*

Mama's like
    mud pies
        in the backyard of 285 Woodman Street.

Mama's like
    coloring books painted
        Black like me.

Mama's like
    the wind that inspires the eagle
        to fly free.

Mama's like
    the giving tree
        growing infinitely.

Mama's like
    the *Bump,* the *Jerk,*
        and the *Rock Steady.*

Mama's like
    Tubby Tales and
        memories of Missouri.

Mama's like
    a melody
        in the sweet sounds of poetry.

Mama's like laughs
    Mama's like grace
        Mama's like sun shining on my face.
Mama's like dance
    Mama's like free
        Mama's like precious
Mama's like me.

I Cry

*In dedication to
Two warring countries
One people*

My voice cries the river Nile
to liberate myself,
torn between myself.

I cry Ethiopia
to cleanse the pain
of my heart's humiliation.

I cry Eritrea
to heal the hurt
of my soul's degradation.

Foreigners
wearing a mask of peace,
penetrate deep into the heart
of my womb.

Waging war
on my homeland,
leaving scars upon my spirit.

Dividing
one family.
Father suppresses mother,

Sisters become strangers,
nameless, faceless,
brothers become enemies.

Now my mind,
body and soul
reawaken to the truth,

That you are me,
and I am you.
I am my brother's keeper,

Stand together to ascend.
Who waged this war upon us?
Not us, but together we will win.

No hands
can keep us warring with ourselves.
Let our hearts beat in tune,

Playing in harmony
the rhythm of our ancestors.
The river Nile runs through our veins.

Our blood pulses
like an ignited flame.
We are the luminance of the Nubian sun,

Moving towards freedom,
triumphing towards freedom,
Singing, dancing, each step towards liberation.

Ugye ashe nefku inay iskahun ti te ne fis alleh.
Ugh sija si'irka skab he g, ine ber alleju.
Ashe nifen iskajun be fikir allen.

Come hade TeTew ilna.
Come hizbi te jaba beerna.
Hade le bi, hade hizbi.

I win, you're still breathing.
You win, I am still living.
We win, we are still loving.

AS ONE, WE ARE STILL STANDING.
United as one,
One heart, one people.

Call to the Brothas

Your hisses, heys, whistles, and stares
don't greet me with comfort.
Brotha lookin' at me like
I'm some tasty side dish to be served
to satisfy his lustful appetite.

So I look to the sky and try to become invisible,
while he prepares to devour me with drunken eyes,
that search my entire body for satisfaction.
And I am made to sacrifice my sacredness.

No wonder why so many of us dress like them.
It is a trip how their words can make this body
feel so worthless.
What is left of me as I walk by
is a feeling of disgust.

In him, in me, in men, and then
as I begin to pick my spirit up
from the floor where it was left,
I hear in the distance...

"Hey, Hey Bitch. Daaamn you know you fiiine as a mothafucka!" And "Umm Umm, look at that ASS!"

Oh am I supposed to take your disrespect
as a compliment?
Do you really think
I like to be called out my name?
Ain't that a shame.

All these babies, sons, daddies, grandpas
rapin' my Divinity, takin' my womb in vain.
As if I were someone's welcome mat
to carelessly step on and off of
and you add to yesterday's foul and filthy stains.

I mean I can't even walk down the block
without some old ass man rollin' up 'side me
talkin' 'bout, *"Hey li'l mama, you sho' is fine.
Need a ride?"*

HELL NO, I'm thinking, as I turn my face to the side,
to escape his sinful smile.
All the while I'm ready to run like lightning
'cause in any second he could pull me into the back
of his dirty ol' Cadillac.

Hell how am I so sure he won't?
What in his right mind would make him want to stop
for a 7, 8, 9, 10, 11, 12, 13 year old GIRL anyway?!!!
The thought of this brings me so much pain

Knowing at the end of each day
I must reembrace my feminine essence.
The one that created he
who disrespects me in his presence.

And you wonder **WHY?** I cross to the other side
And you wonder **WHY?** I don't speak
And you wonder **WHY?** I got an attitude
Because I am tired of being made your

BITCH!

400 Years of Lynching and Counting

Crystal tears
clear disillusionment in hopeless eyes.
Stains of struggle
marked on Black faces
erases with time and forgiveness.
Still southern trees bearing strange fruit
are not forgotten.

Men, women, Black boys' and girls' bodies
swaying in a gentle breeze.
The scent of fire rising at the knees.
Hot summer day,
Ice cold faces fixed.
While heartache beats inside a mother's chest,
flames consume her baby's last breath.

Three Blacks beaten
kidnapped for rape.
Bones crack against iron paddles
by fists full of hate.
White claimed Black made sexual passes
so death fits the fate,
for any male who wears a Black face.

Father defends daughter,
killed the White man who stole her virginity,
a young thirteen.
Confusion of a White man's lust mixed with hate,
tore away her delicate womb
leaving an empty space.

Father avenged,
his victory short lived.
The angry mob attacked him.
Made an example of those who dared to protest,
slowly they cut away his humanly flesh.

These sorrow songs go on
like an everlasting melody.
With each lullaby I cry
and hear the wailing harmony.
400 years of lynching and counting.
Of souls deemed soulless
proclaiming their humanity.

Question

Learn to question.
Deconstruct institutions
of miseducation,
that X out our existence,
wipe away traces of Blackness,
alter our senses.
Cause Black children
to despise their ebony reflection.
"I ain't no African!"
'Cause Black by definition
be wicked, evil and sullen.
Images of beauty hidden behind
blue eyes and platinum hair dyes
are lies.
Realize the time we livin' in,
mass self-destruction,
soul corruption.
Self-hate be the #1 killer.
Now I place chains around my neck
and proudly call myself a nigger.
Who am I?
Pimp, Player, Hustler
Who am I?
Prisoner, cotton picker on a penal plantation
Who am I?

Ghetto superstar,
possessed by dollar signs
and big time corporations
Who am I?
MVP. Played by owners branding me as property
Who am I?
Neo slave
Sold my soul to a new age slave trade,
bought and sold by the American dream,
dollars and cream.
Cash rules everything around me,
Bling Bling.
Look at us in the US,
jewels dress the necks of Black innocents,
at the expense
of a South African child,
sentenced to death
in gold mines that stole his brilliance.
Is this success?
To measure our worth by material wealth.
Model ourselves after master and mistress.
The blood on our hands drips ancestral memories,
of a stolen people, land and legacy.
We've journeyed centuries
in search of self.

Struggling to survive
and still we rise
against the odds of life,
where hopes are defied
by broken dreams
and empty stomachs swollen from poverty.
My people keep on, keep on, keep on moving.
But be moving in the right direction.
Ask one question,
Are we taking the path towards freedom?
Or blindly being led towards self-destruction?

My nephew, Khalil

Black On Black Love

Come my Brown Ebony Sunshine
What could be better than Black on Black love?
One man, One woman, together.
Plant seeds of infinite possibilities
Blossom into gardens of maturity
With tender touches, thoughtful words and honesty.

Come my honey chocolate dream
Into the sweetness of my serenity.
Come inside my soft embrace
To taste bliss wrapped up in your blackness
Utter words of forgiveness.

Let pain drift away like grey rain clouds
'Cause you and I can weather *any* storm.
For more than centuries we've endured
Burdens of heartache and self-hate.
Still we stand, Black womb of Black man,
As one, steadily on the rise.

'Cause I have not lost faith in your stride,
I see the light of hope in your eyes.
Exalt me as you climb
And I'll carry you to your heights
Body, spirit and mind.

Transcend space and time
So all that is left is you and I
Redefine ourselves in love's endless rhyme.
Something poetic, powerful and prophetic,
Unique and authentic.
Black love reawakened with patience, respect and reverence.

Let's walk the path of righteousness – hand in hand –
Vowing to protect this sacred union
Of Black woman, Black man.
Life's beginnings began in Black love.
We be the origins of humanity
And I bear witness to the beauty of its legacy

Flowering ever gracefully inside me
Nestled in my being.
Black brilliance we be shining indestructibly
Like the moon and sun, come stand as one
'Cause we've been since love's conception
One body, one mind, one *Soul Divine Reflection!*

*Artwork by
Larry Hollins,
my father.*

Sherche Yamaika Page

Inspired by "Honey, I Love"

Only When It's Dark Enough Can You See the Stars

I wanna be a star
shining like blackness in the summer sun.
I wanna be the illuminated one,
offering brilliance to the night sky.
My twinkling touch will taste sweet
like chocolate kisses.

I will be the universe's spirit song,
calling all my children home.
Their sullen eyes will gaze up in wonder
and remember their majesty.
I wanna be their ancient wisdom,
their hope for liberation.

I wanna be 'cause in a world of material obsession,
stars drive fancy cars and run from revolution.
I wanna *be* cause where I'm from,
stars are plated in gold and placed in cement tombs
on Hollywood Blvd., where homeless men,
women and children lie wondering why this star
never shined their light upon them.

I *wanna* be 'cause where I live,
stars are those whose pockets are full,
yet whose hearts are empty.

I wanna be 'cause when I was young,
stars were given to those privileged two,
who were given too much and came too few.

I wanna *be* 'cause where I've been,
the kind of star I hope to be, quickly
becomes a forgotten memory.
As babies bounce to stagnant beats
Of Dr. Dre and Puff Daddy.
As sacred women and girls
Give up the GODDESS to back that thang up.

As sickly bodies sell their children for crystal rocks
on dilapidated street corners. And sons do time
for sellin' the poison, which put their mamas
in a crack fiend's prison-paradise.
These painful pictures leave tear stains in my eyes,
as I see worthless dollars being worshipped
in exchange for brilliant minds.

Yet I know of a light that shines everlasting
inside our souls,
lost in a modern day trade of self for slave.
Us daughters and sons breathe blackness
and await rebirth, to rise from our depths
into our ascension.
Our revelation to the world has never been far,
but only when it's dark enough can you see the stars.

I Am

I am
  love
    life
      light
All things limitless
  Lyrically profound
    Gifted wise
      Intelligent

Black
  African
    Warrior woman
God child
  Conceived of Divinity
    Birthed of the Nile

Serene like still waters
  Searing like a wild fire,
    I ignite
      Complexity
Simply can't define me
  I can't be confined see
    I am like breath to life
      The essence of all things

Moving
  Inspiring
    Captivating
Awakening
  Silent words
    to let truth be heard
      Across continents

From prison yards to synagogues
  City blocks to hilltops
    LA to New Yorkers
Freedom fighters to soul searchers
  From rich to poor to exiled beggars
    From child to elder
      This message be forever

Unifying
  Defying
    Testifying
Uprising
  Against the presence of ignorance
    Idleness can't crush the spirit of resistance

WE THE PEOPLE

Are one soul in this movement
  One voice in this message

WE THE PEOPLE

Are one vein
   Refusing to fall slain

To sexism, oppression
   Capitalistic racism

WE THE PEOPLE

Birth visions of freedom
   Remembering

Malcolm's,
   Woodson's,
     Harriet's,
       Turner's,
         Martin's,
Garvey's,
   Delaney's,
     Sojourner's
       Ancestral warriors,
         Eternal freedom soldiers

Those who fought
  with bellowing cries
    And died with dignity
      on the front lines
We honor your legacy
  Pay homage to your memory
    Through heart love
      make change

The future of revolution uprises today,
  in spirits and minds
    We are the light that shines
      Brightly inside ancestral eyes
We are revelations of ancient prayers
  We are descendants of hope's persistent past
    Making freedom's dream
      Reality at last!

Sherehe Yamaisha Rozé means "celebration of life's rose." Me in my father's hands at four months old.

Somos Una Gente

Somos una gente.
Rooted in the memory of Mandinga, Mende and Kush.
We push forward, upward like branches.
Demanding recognition, remembrance.
We are Nubia's sunkissed descendants.
Speaking languages built on ancient civilizations.
Whose lyric, scripted in Olmec monuments, teach us,
never to forget the mother tongue that birthed us.

Brought us to las Américas by Bering Strait journeys,
and currents carrying, mariner tribes, world travelers,
traders, explorers.
Before we were captured, bought and sold,
shackled to sugar cane and cotton fields.
Filling the greedy bellies of foreign economic interests.
Before we were sambo, zambo, mammy, memín,
mulatto, half-breed,
we were Xi, Olmec, Toltec, Aztec, African,
civilization's foundation.

Our ancestors calendared constellations with
mathematical precision.
Originated science and medicine, molded
from the earth.
Their hands shaped nature into aesthetic masterpieces.
Sculpting history into step pyramids
and terracotta faces.

Chiseled with corn rows, and curved hips,
full lips and round noses,
in ode to our Black beauty and humanity.

While studying Español in México I asked my teacher,
Why is this Jesus statued with black skin,
pure as midnight?
He replied, "Because it has worn old from time,
it's lost its shine",
But I knew better.
Because before the bandera was wrapped
in colors del conquístador,
el blanco y el rojo, there was el Negro.

And their black and bronzed colors and broad features,
are etched in the faces of México,
woven in the history of México,
spoken in the lyric of México,
practiced in the faith of México,
seen in the spirit and soul of México,
danced in the folklore of México,
tasted in the sabor of México.
Because we are México, siempre, antiguo,
presente y futuro!

We are present in the rhythms of instruments
bearing African origins,
el marimbol, y cajon.
Los corridos, known as the heart songs of México,
were born of struggle and resistance,

narrating a people's opposition to indifference.
El Zapateado y ballet folklórico Veracruzano,
dances La Bamba, in homage to Mbamba,
the Angolan town from which
their ancestors descended.

To learn Español is to remember El Moro.
Los Africanos who ruled Spain for 800 years.
Gave us their Arabic words,
barrio, limón, arroz, cero, azúcar, azul, adobe, chisme,
café and 40,000 others.
Their presence moves through art, arches and flamenco.
So to say I am Spanish, I must say I am African.

To say yo soy Mexicana, I must say, yo soy La Indígena,
el Español, el Asiático, la Africana, y mucho mas.
Porque somos una gente!
They named me la tercera raíz, the forgotten third root.
But I am not invisible.
I can be seen breathing, smiling, becoming,
within every city of mi tierra linda.
From Veracruz to Guerrero,
from Oaxaca to Sonora,
from Ensenada to Sinaloa.

I am the daughter of kings, queens, slaves, and
cimarrones, defying injustice!
I am the independence fought by Mexico's
second president,
Vicente Guerrero, the Black warrior!

I am the rebellion of Gaspar Yanga, fleeing oppression,
forming the first freedmen's town in the face of slavery!
I am the resistance born of self-determination,
won on battlefields,
in the names of Morelos, Juarez, Zapata, and the
4,000 soldiers of Puebla!

Why should Cinco de Mayo and Mexican history
matter to me?
Porque somos una gente, whose blood has been
shared and shed
In the name of sisterhood and brotherhood.
Once before, there existed no borders between us.
Somos familia, and I seek to reclaim the parts of me
they tried to divide and conquer.
Hermanos, stand with me, united and remember,
that we are one!

Gente, rooted in the memory of
Mandinga, Mende and Kush.
Pushing forward, upward like branches.
Demanding recognition, remembrance.
We are Nubia's sunkissed descendants.
Speaking languages built on ancient civilizations.
Whose lyric, scripted in Olmec monuments, teach us,
never to forget the mother tongue that birthed us!

About the Author

Sherehe Yamaisha Rozé is an award winning artist, writer, photographer, dancer and educator. She has authored poetry, and performed at cultural events, bookstores, schools, colleges, universities, national conferences, theatres and on television since the age of four. Sherehe graduated from San Diego Mesa College with an Associate of Arts degree in Selected Studies. She received her Bachelor of Arts degree in African American Studies from the University of California, Berkeley, and earned her Master of Arts degree in Education from National University. Sherehe's mission is to enlighten, uplift and motivate others to seek knowledge of self and self-love. Sherehe lectures and provides trainings throughout the country on how to create and integrate culturally relevant curricula into the classroom. Her work connects the human family. Her words carry a universal message of inspiration that encourages people to recognize and manifest their limitless potential.